Making
Strategy
Work

The Lessons Learned Series

Wondering how the most accomplished leaders from around the globe have tackled their toughest challenges? Now you can find out—with Lessons Learned. Concise and engaging, each volume in this new series offers twelve to fourteen insightful essays by top leaders in business, the public sector, and academia on the most pressing issues they've faced.

A crucial resource for today's busy executive, Lessons Learned gives you instant access to the wisdom and expertise of the world's most talented leaders.

Other Books in the series:

Leading by Example

Managing Change

Managing Your Career

Managing Conflict

Starting a Business

Hiring and Firing

Making the Sale

Executing for Results

Sparking Innovation

Making Strategy Work

LES50NS

Boston, Massachusetts

Printed in the United States of America
12 11 10 09 08   5 4 3 2 1

Library of Congress Cataloging-in-Publication Data

Making strategy work.
        p. cm. — (Lessons learned)
    1. Strategic planning.
    HD30.28.M327 2008
    658.4'012—dc22

                                2008022293

⊰ A NOTE FROM THE ⊱
PUBLISHER

In partnership with Fifty Lessons, a leading
provider of digital media content, Harvard
Business School Press is pleased to an-
nounce the launch of Lessons Learned, a
new book series that showcases the trusted
voices of the world's most experienced leaders. Through the power of personal storytelling, each book in this series presents the
accumulated wisdom of some of the world's
best-known experts, and offers insights into
how these individuals think, approach new
challenges, and use hard-won lessons from
experience to shape their leadership phi-
losophies. Organized thematically, accord-
ing to the topics at the top of managers'
agendas—leadership, change management,
entrepreneurship, innovation, and strategy,
to name a few—each book draws from Fifty
Lesson's extensive video library of inter-
views with CEOs and other thought leaders.

A Note from the Publisher

Here, the world's leading senior executives, academics, and business thinkers speak directly and candidly about their triumphs and defeats. Taken together, these powerful stories offer the advice you'll need to take on tomorrow's challenges.

We invite you to join the conversation now. You'll find both new ways of looking at the world, and the tried-and-true advice you need to illuminate the path forward.

❧ CONTENTS ❧

Contents

Contents

———◆◆◆———

Communicate Your Strategy Clearly

———◆◆◆———

Sanjiv Ahuja

Chairman, Orange

WHEN YOU'RE LEADING a business, an enterprise, or any other endeavor that involves a large number of people, the best way to get results from them is to make sure that the expectation you set for them is simple, understandable, and comprehensible across the board.

Making Strategy Work

Orange operates in sixteen countries. We have more than thirty-three thousand people, and unless a business like ours has a very simple, comprehensible, and executable strategy, it is very hard not only to get the buy in from the team, but it's even harder to get it executed.

As a leader, it's very simple: set the goal. Set the strategy to be very simple—as simple as you can make it. The way I look at it, if you can articulate your strategy in a one-minute elevator ride or put it on a single piece of paper—and that too without a lot of commas or semicolons in how you describe it—then you have a strategy that can be executed and worked upon. Make sure you don't use any buzzwords in that strategy—especially in our industry—and don't use any techno-geeky stuff that we're all enamored of. Make it very simple, comprehensible, and as crisp as you possibly can, and then your team can work on it.

Take the example of Orange strategy. It is a very large document that we generated after a lot of work—a lot of detailed work. It's very

Communicate Your Strategy Clearly

customer-centric, as it ought to be, but it is not a document that can be understood by thirty-three thousand employees of Orange.

I need the help, participation, execution, effort, and energy of every single one of them focused on that strategy. So the first thing we did—and what we're doing now—is making it very understandable and saying, "These are the parameters within Orange, what our strategy is all about, what we expect [everyone] to do day in and day out."

Each one of them has a different role to play in the delivery of that strategy. It is imperative that we take the essence of that document and put it on a single sheet of paper in a very understandable, simple manner that every one of our employees can understand, and can look at what role they can or should play in the execution and delivery of that strategy.

Unless you can put that clarity in your goals, you cannot expect the execution to be world class. One of the things I've always focused on is keeping the goals and the objectives simple and understandable. The minute you take that away, the execution becomes very, very hard.

TAKEAWAYS

- ⚐ The best way to get results from people when you're leading a business is to ensure that the set expectation is simple, understandable, and comprehensible across the board.

- ⚐ You should be able to articulate your strategy on a single piece of paper. The language should be simple and crisp, not filled with buzzwords or other "techno-geeky" stuff, so that employees can easily understand their roles.

- ⚐ If you cannot put that clarity in your goals, you cannot expect world-class execution.

The Impact of Strategic Storytelling

Jay Conger

Henry Kravis Research Chair Professor, Kravis Leadership Institute, Claremont McKenna College

ONE OF THE most important mediums you and I have as leaders is that of communicating through stories. I like to call them strategic stories, because in many ways they're stories with a strategic end in mind.

Making Strategy Work

They're a powerful tool that many managers and executives forget to deploy. My point is that if you want recall—if you want your staff to remember the genuine priorities or remember why we're going in a certain direction—they need stories to help remind them of that reason, purpose, or type of decision they have to take.

Let me illustrate this idea of strategic stories with a story. This is a story that Herb Kelleher—one of the founders of Southwest Airlines in the United States and its former CEO and chairman—used to tell as he traveled around the United States, visiting his operations. It was a story that in part explained who the competitors to Southwest Airlines were, as well as being a story to illustrate why Southwest priced its tickets so low, because Southwest Airlines was famous for its low-priced tickets.

What he would do in meetings with people from Southwest—and even with customers—is say, "It's funny; I get letters all the time from shareholders, and they're often angry letters. They say, 'America West

The Impact of Strategic Storytelling

is flying between Los Angeles and Las Vegas for $149 one way. And you, Herb Kelleher, at Southwest, are pricing $79 for that same one-way ticket. Don't you have the decency to at least kick your price up to $129? Why are you leaving so much on the table?'

"Well, what I do is write back and reply, 'Thank you so much for your letter. However, you don't really understand who we are, and you really don't understand who our competition is. It's the automobile; it's not other airlines. And $79 is the price to drive, including maintenance, insurance, and gasoline, from Los Angeles to Las Vegas. That's how we price our tickets.'"

He would use that simple story to drive home what in many ways could be seen as the entire strategy of the organization, vis-à-vis its competition. But it was done in such a way that everyone at Southwest, all the way down to the baggage handler, knew who the competitors were and why that ticket was priced the way it was.

The primary lesson learned is that stories have enormous power in terms of recall. If you look at statistics, at PowerPoint [presentations], or at documents, what you discover from all the research is that there's almost no recall. So you can use all the PowerPoint [slides], statistical presentations, or handouts you want, but almost none of that will be remembered. What will be remembered are a few compelling stories that you share with your organization and with your team. Those will guide them when they're far away from you, which by the way is much of the day.

How do you craft a good strategic story? Well, what we know is that the stories you and I might tell in a work context are different from the stories we might tell our family at dinner, or tell our children when we're putting them to bed. The first characteristic is they're short—very short. Anywhere from one-and-a-half to two-and-a-half minutes is about all anybody can retain as a listener, so keep your stories short. Second, they shouldn't have more than two or three characters at most. The more characters, the more difficult it is to remember the story. Third, keep it simple. Build it around a singular message you wish to convey. Fourth, tell it as if it's actually happening in the present tense. We know that when you do that, it brings the listeners into the story and they actually participate within it. Next, make certain you have got a few visual images, because we store visual images far more deeply. A picture is worth thousands of words. Make sure the images you share in the story tie into the theme you want everyone to remember. Finally, if you can, repeat a word or phrase that is the essence of your message.

TAKEAWAYS

⚔ Communicating through strategic storytelling is a powerful tool that leaders often forget to employ.

Making Strategy Work

⚜ For employees to remember priorities and execute strategy, they need stories to remind them of the decisions they have to make.

⚜ To craft a strong strategy story, keep it short and simple, limit the number of characters, include visuals, and tell the story in the present tense.

Setting Clear and Achievable Goals

Roger Parry

Former Chairman and CEO,
Clear Channel International

SETTING GOALS FROM the perspective of a chief executive really is another way of asking a question about strategy, because the people reporting to a chief executive need to know what's expected of them. The important thing is to have a thorough understanding of the issues facing a business and the environment within which it's operating. As a result of having an understanding of that environment, you can then set meaningful goals for the management.

Let me give you an example. If you have, as I do, a business that operates in more than fifty countries, it doesn't necessarily follow that each general manager has exactly the same goal. For our business in China, for example, there is an enormous opportunity to grow, so the goal for the guy running the Chinese business unit is to look for new investments and ways of putting money to work.

If you take the other end of the extreme—which in my case would be Switzerland, where the market is completely mature and satisfied—the goal there for the general manager is about operating efficiency. He is looking to do the same amount of business in a more effective way, whereas his Chinese counterpart is simply looking to do more business. The lesson is that setting clear goals comes from a thorough understanding of the business environment in which you are operating.

Another important consideration—and it's a word that I don't think appears in

Setting Clear and Achievable Goals

English—is "do-ability." By this I mean, is a goal actually achievable? One of the worst things you can do is to say to an operating manager, "Here is your goal," and the operating manager then looks at you and says, "Such a thing is impossible."

We are all familiar with that in our daily lives. If you say to a child, "I want you to jump over a ten-meter hurdle," the child obviously knows he can't do it and will be upset. In the same way, if you set, as people do sometimes, business goals that are wholly unachievable, it may make the chief executive feel very macho and tough that he's set for people an enormous stretch target—but if the target is unachievable, the only result is going to be disappointed managers and a general feeling of failure.

Some years ago I was working in an advertising agency group and was responsible for one of the public relations businesses we'd recently acquired. The chief executive told us that he wanted this business to double its sales within two years. Now, the problem with doubling your sales within two years in a business like that is that you have to go and hire people to do the work. The constraint actually wasn't winning new clients; the constraint was hiring people, because at the time there was a great shortage.

So we went away from that annual budget review knowing in advance that we were going to fail, because it wasn't going to be possible to hire that number of people sufficiently quickly. The same goal had been set for all the businesses across the whole group, so we were stuck with something we couldn't possibly achieve.

If what went wrong was the original process of setting the goal, everyone has to admit to that and be realistic about it. If you don't have that sort of postmortem, the problem you'll face is that you'll get so many disaffected members of staff that your whole organization becomes dysfunctional. There will be a lot of people working, feeling this sense of failure. It is very important that people feel a sense of success.

That does not mean that you always set goals that are so easy that everyone achieves them. It's not like an examination process where everybody passes. The important thing is that where a goal is missed, it's missed for reasons that everyone understands and you can genuinely say, "That was force majeure; that was an external unexpected event." It shouldn't be missed because the original goal was so unrealistic that it couldn't be done.

Clear goals for a business manager come as a result of understanding the environment within which they're operating, and also as a result of a dialogue between that business manager and his or her chief executive. The right goals are those that both parties understand and buy in to, rather than something that just sounds like a very good number to talk about to your shareholders.

TAKEAWAYS

⊣ Setting goals is another way of asking a question about strategy. To do that, you need a thorough understanding of the issues the business faces and the environment in which it operates.

- ⚅ Also necessary is for the goals to be achievable. Otherwise, the results will be feelings of disappointment and failure. Be careful, however, not to set goals that are easily achievable by everyone.

- ⚅ The right goals are understood and bought in to by managers and executives, and not goals that just sound like good numbers to share with stakeholders.

If You're Not Getting Better, You're Getting Worse

David Brandon

Chairman and CEO, Domino's Pizza

I WAS INFLUENCED by my experience early in my adult life as a college football player at a high level. One of the things I observed during that period was that I was a part of a very successful program. We won virtually every game. We won the championship every year, and yet we were a bunch of eighteen- to twenty-one-year-old kids who could easily have developed an attitude that we were so good and so successful that we didn't need to work hard or prepare; all we needed to do was to show up, and we would win.

I observed how great coaches handle a very interesting dynamic like that, because it happens in business all the time. You have a great quarter or two, you're doing very well against your budgets and plans, the media is writing all kinds of nice things about you, and the easiest thing you can do is to back off and start to believe that it's all going to happen automatically. The way the coaches dealt with it was by drumming into our heads a fundamental belief system that you either get better or you get worse; things never stay the same. We heard that over and over and over again. You cannot stay the same; you're either going to get better or you're going to get worse.

If You're Not Getting Better

Once we began to believe that as a team, we understood that it didn't matter whether next Saturday we were going into the game favored to win by forty points. It didn't matter. What mattered was that we had to get better, we had to perform at a higher level as benchmarked against how we performed in the previous games, because we truly believed—the coaches helped us to believe—that if we weren't getting better, we were going to get worse. There wasn't an opportunity for us to simply stay the same and live in a static situation.

I took that learning, went into business, and I observed over and over again situations where organizations become complacent. They become apathetic. They believe that everything they touch is going to turn to gold, and that all they have to do is hand out their business card, talk a little bit about who they are and their track record for success, and good things are going to happen. Invariably, those are the companies that fail, because they don't understand the concept of either getting better or getting worse; they try to stay the same.

One of the things that I do over and over again at my organization is to reinforce the concept that we have to get better, that even during times of tremendous success, if we get complacent and start to read the press clippings and believe that we're better than we are, we're going to fall back.

One of the concepts that is truly essential if you really want to have a high-performance organization is the concept of continuous improvement. It's almost a cliché, but it really is something that the culture has to embrace, and it has to manifest itself in everyday behavior. The notion is, "I have to figure out a way to do something a little bit better today than I did yesterday." And if you can foster that in the culture of your organization, great things happen.

A big part of it is how you benchmark your results. For many years as a private company, Domino's really benchmarked against itself, without looking at the outside world. We were proud of the fact that for many years we had positive same-store sales, which is a big financial indicator of growth and success in the retail world. Well, that was the good news.

The bad news was that during those same years our competitors were growing at a faster rate. We were actually giving up market share. At the same time, we were hosting internal celebrations of the fact that against our own internal matrix we were doing well. We not only had to look at what had been our past results and reconcile how we were performing against that benchmark, but also we needed to look at the world around us, look at our competitors, and in many instances I really wanted us to look at the very best in class. Who is out there doing the best possible job in this particular area of business? We need to find out what their results are and start to hold ourselves accountable for that particular level of performance.

We accept mediocrity because we can choose a lot of people around us who are just as mediocre as we are. I want to find the very, very best, and I want to benchmark against them, and I want to get as good or better. I think if I lead that expectation and I get my team and my organization to embrace it, that's how we're going to become world-class performers.

———◆◆◆———

TAKEAWAYS

———◆◆◆———

- ⚔ When an organization is successful, people tend to believe that they can stop improving. But things never stay the same: either you get better, or you get worse.

- ⚔ The minute companies become complacent and apathetic is the minute they begin to fail. To have a high-performance organization, you must foster a culture of continuous improvement.

🔀 Don't accept mediocrity. Instead, look to your competitors, and bench-mark yourself against them to achieve world-class performance.

Watch Your Competitors and Challenge Your Strategy

Philip Kotler

S. C. Johnson & Son Professor of International Marketing at the Kellogg School of Management, Northwestern University

I DID SOME work for IBM for some years, but in 1991 I was invited by John Akers to attend the annual board meeting. I found that three-day experience to be fantastic in the presentations that were made. I didn't know of any other company that had asked customers to make presentations, a district manager to make a presentation, and, of all things, a competitor to make a presentation.

Now, you never will invite the CEO of a competitive firm to come to your board meeting. In fact, I don't even know what the legality of that would be. But in any case, IBM wanted to learn about competitors. One of the competitors that concerned IBM a lot was Sun Microsystems.

Sun was headed by Scott McNealy, who was quite a personality. They couldn't invite Scott McNealy. The thought occurred to them that the board members should hear about what a company like Sun Microsystems might be thinking of toward IBM. Someone remembered that a young man working at IBM had formerly been at Sun. It was a practice of companies to invite people from competitive companies and so on, not to get at any secret

they shouldn't know about, but more
just to have the mind-set of a competitive
company.

They asked this young man to do some
research to bring himself up to date about
Sun Microsystems and Scott McNealy.
Then they surprised him afterward by saying they would like him to make a presentation to the board. He thought that meant a
statistical presentation, basically. They said,
"No, we want you to be Scott McNealy. You
almost look like him, anyway. Feel free to
just talk to the board as if you were Scott
McNealy, and tell what you're going to plan
to do to IBM."

He agreed. In fact, he was quite up in
enthusiasm. This all happened before the
event, but I heard that he was very much
looking forward to it.

He was introduced, and the board was
told that they were going to be introduced to
Scott McNealy, or a reasonable facsimile,
to hear from Scott what he was going to
do to IBM.

Making Strategy Work

The young man just looked at the board members, eyed them, and said, "IBM, we're going to bury you. We are a network-centric company. Networks are much more important than hardware. You are a hardware company. Keep doing your hardware. We'll catch up."

The board looked kind of stunned. Then the R&D guy, an important fellow at IBM at the time, said that it was an interesting proposition. But frankly, he didn't think this person—Scott McNealy—really understood that it was growing the speed and the capacity of the hardware, the horsepower, that would make all the difference to [IBM's] customers.

That led to a little debate, but it was won by the R&D guy. I think that set back IBM ten years. I say ten years because when Lou Gerstner took over the company and made all those changes, one of the things he said toward the end was that IBM was a network-centric company.

TAKEAWAYS

- ⧉ To better understand strategy, it's vital to get feedback from your customers, your managers, and your competitors.

- ⧉ More importantly, when you get such feedback, take the time to listen to it.

- ⧉ Proceeding with the status quo or moving forward on false assumptions can lead to significant setbacks.

———◀▸◀▸———

Teach Managers How to Think, Not What to Think

Clayton Christensen

Robert and Jane Cizik Professor of Business Administration, Harvard Business School

———◀▸◀▸———

I CAME BACK to academia as a forty-year-old doctoral student. I developed this model from my research that showed that what cripples successful companies is rarely that somebody comes into their own market with a better product but rather that somebody comes in at the bottom of the market with an inexpensive, simple product that caters only to the needs of the least-demanding customers. And then they move up.

What we showed is that, over and over again, when a well-run company focuses on listening to its customers and investing where profit margins are most attractive, those paradigms of good management that they follow help the leaders move up-market but paralyze them when somebody comes from down below. And they just can't attack below.

Here's an example: Toyota attacked the American market, not by making Lexuses but with this crummy, little, rusty subcompact model called the Corona in the 1960s. Then they moved up-market to Tercels, Corollas, Camrys, Avalons, and Forerunners. And then they made Lexuses.

Every once in a while, the leaders in the industry—General Motors and Ford—would look down at Toyota coming up at them and say, "We ought to go compete against those guys." And so they'd send down a Chevette or a Pinto. But then they'd compare the profitability of those little subcompacts with the profitability of a big Ford Explorer or a Cadillac Escalade, and it actually didn't make economic sense. This phenomenon I labeled "disruption."

An engineer in the middle of Intel read an early academic paper that we'd written on this. She said that after she read it, she looked down at the bottom of the microprocessor market and there was Syrex coming at Intel. Syrex had already picked off the entry-level computer business—the processors in those entry-level computers—and they were coming up. Intel was fleeing up-market.

I knew nothing about the microprocessor business, but she arranged, through a series of events, ultimately to give me a meeting with Andy Grove, the [Intel] chairman, and his executive staff. That was a once-in-a-lifetime opportunity for a no-name professor like me.

Making Strategy Work

Grove is a very down-to-business sort of a guy. He said, "Just give me ten minutes and tell me what this means for Intel, and we'll be onto our other stuff."

I said, "Andy, I can't do it in ten minutes; I need thirty. Let me just describe this model of disruption that's emerged from my research, and then let's talk about what it means for Intel." He sat back impatiently.

I was ten minutes into describing this model, and he cut me off and said, "I got it. Tell me what it means for Intel." He summarized what he understood of the model, and he actually did get it very well.

I said, "Andy, I just need ten more minutes because I'd like to describe how this process of disruption worked its way through a very different industry than microprocessors, and then we'll talk about Intel." So he sat back impatiently again.

I decided I'd tell him the story about how in the steel industry, steel minimills had picked off rebar at the bottom of the market and then had moved up-market, and the integrated steel companies had retreated to higher- and higher-margin products. I picked steel because it was very different from microprocessors, so Andy wouldn't get confused at all, but in many ways it was a perfect analogy to what I thought was going to happen in microprocessors.

When I finished telling the story about steel, Andy said, "I get it. So what it means for Intel is . . ." And he got it. I've thought since, if I had been suckered into telling Andy Grove what I thought he ought to do in the microprocessor business, I would have just been crucified. There's no way I would have the knowledge to overpower his wisdom about that business. But instead of teaching him what to think, I taught him how to think, and he could reach his own conclusion. Once he'd reached his own conclusion, I didn't have to convince him.

That has been a powerful lesson for me. And subsequent to that, I get several people every day who somehow crowd onto my calendar because they have an idea for a new growth business. As they ask for my advice, rather than telling them what I think they should think, I always pull one of these models about innovation that's emerged from my research that I think is appropriate to them. I'll describe the model for them, and then I'll show how this process worked its way through another industry. What I find is that just over and over again, they say, "I get it. So what it means for me is this . . ."

TAKEAWAYS

- Rarely do successful companies get crippled because a company comes into their market with a better product.

- Instead, competitors come in with a simple, inexpensive product that caters to the least-demanding customers, and then they move up-market.

Teach Managers How to Think

⚐ Meanwhile, in a phenomenon called "disruption," the industry leaders may make minimal attempts to compete against this new entrant, but ultimately they instead focus on profitability and never see the competition coming.

Finding the Flowers Among the Weeds

Lynda Gratton

*Professor of Management Practice,
London Business School*

THIS IS AN old story. I guess I must have
been about twenty-six years old, and it
was my very first year as a consultant. I was
working for one of the big consulting practices, and I remember we all went to Ireland

to advise a company about their long-term
strategy.

Like any great consultants at that stage,
what we did was to ask everybody to get into
a room, and then we said to them, "Let's
think about what this organization could
be like in ten years' time." Over the space
of a day, we filled up about fifty flip charts
with all the things that they could do for the
future.

That was all great; we were really ener-
getic, and there were lots of ideas. Then, at
the end of the day, we stood in the middle
of the room and looked around. There
must have been two hundred things that we
could do in the future. And it struck me so
forcibly then—and actually it's been a huge
learning for me—that there just isn't any
reason to generate masses of ideas like that.
What you have to do is to know, of all the
things that you can really work on, what the
one, two, or maybe three or four things are
that are really going to make a difference.

I guess for me it's a bit like saying that
the garden is full of weeds, and some of

Finding Flowers Among the Weeds

the weeds are actually flowers, but how do you know which ones they are? Of all the things that you can do, which are the four things that will really make a difference to your organization? Thinking back on that, the lesson for me was that you just have to focus. You absolutely have to focus. There are so many things you can do, so you have to just focus on the three or four things that will make a difference.

But how do you do that? Well, those three or four things have to be very tightly aligned to what it is you're trying to do as an organization. They have to be aligned to your business strategy. They have to be big things—things that, when employees look at them, they say, "I feel really excited about that; I feel really engaged in that." I guess for me, the capacity to know what's a weed and what's a flower is really one of the most important things I ever learned.

I've engaged with organizations many times in blue sky thinking, but what I learned was that while having that many ideas was great, you had to find a way of synthesizing and filtering them down. The question is, how do you do that? I guess there are many ways, but the way that I learned to do it is by setting up a three-by-three grid. On one axis, I asked the executives, "How important do you think this is to the long-term success of this organization: very important, important, or not particularly important?" Then we went back to the same items, and I said, "Thinking about that item, where are you now? Are you already doing that, have you started doing it, or haven't you even thought about it?"

What we then got was this wonderful matrix. In the top right-hand corner were things that were very important for the long-term future but that people weren't doing anything about right now. We called those the areas of risk, and I think that's a great way of distilling from a large amount of data right down to things that are important. The reason they're really important is that they are things that are important to you for the future, but they are things that you are not doing now.

TAKEAWAYS

- When looking to the future, avoid generating masses of ideas. Focus instead on the handful of ideas that will make a true difference.

- Doing this successfully requires focus. Align those key ideas with the business strategy in a way that employees can become excited and engaged.

- Identify those ideas that are important to the organization for the future, but that you're not working on now, as areas of risk.

Tightening Your Market Niche Can Have Positive Results for Your Business

Mary Cantando

Founder, WomanBusinessOwner.com

ALTHOUGH IT MAY seem counterintuitive, I really believe that tightening your market niche not only can improve your profitability but also can help you to grow your bottom line. I actually have a story to prove this.

Back in the late nineties, I was part of a team that built and sold two technology businesses. After we sold our second business, I decided what I really wanted to do for the rest of my life was not build a team and facilities and deal with all the headaches of a true big business.

I wanted to start just a small, simple business, solving a problem that I thought I had the ability to solve—enabling entrepreneurs to get new *Fortune* 1000 accounts. I set up a business to do this—just this—and by mid-2001, I had a successful business going with a variety of clients.

Then September 11 hit, and, of course, that changed everything for a lot of us. Everybody I have found has a September 11th story, but I have a September 12th story. I woke up on the morning of September 12th, and I was lying in bed thinking about the events of the day before and how they were going to impact everything in my life.

My thoughts rolled around to the client I was going to work with that day, and

Tightening Your Market Niche

I thought, I really did not enjoy working with this guy. Then I thought back to September 11th again, and it occurred to me, "Mary, why would you ever, ever, ever wake up in the morning to spend an entire day working with a client you just felt out of sync with, one whom you didn't truly enjoy working with?"

I put on my slippers, and I padded across the hall to my home office, sat down at my desk, and drew a line down a piece of paper. On the left side of the page, I listed all the clients I truly loved working with. On the right side, I listed all the clients I was putting up with just for the sake of revenue. And it just so happened that everyone on the left side of the page was a woman entrepreneur, and on the right side of the page were all my other clients.

I said to myself, "Mary, this is a sign. This is a sign about what you should be doing with your life." I put pencil to paper, figured out that the clients I was just putting up with were responsible for about 70 percent of my revenue. I took a deep breath, and I picked up the phone and started calling them one after another after another, and

I transferred all those clients to other consulting firms that I had previously considered to be my direct competitors.

The bottom-line result of that was [this]: I get up every day excited about the client I'm going to work with that day. I only work with clients I truly love, and this has made a tremendous difference in my business and my life. From a pure business perspective, what I found is by tightening my leash like this, I've been able to control my sales and marketing costs because I only have to attend a certain number of conferences a year; I only participate in a certain number of national organizations where my clients are.

I rebranded my company to WomanBusinessOwner.com, and I was startled to find in 2001 that the URL was available. No one even got that this was such a distinct market that they would reserve it.

So as a result of rebranding my company, I was actually able to make myself very available to women who were looking for someone doing what I do and for the media so they could access me easily. The bottom line has been a dramatic difference in my profitability and my revenue. And every day, I wake up excited about what I'm doing and whom I'm working with.

———◆———

TAKEAWAYS

———◆———

- ⚜ To grow your bottom line, tighten your market niche, even if it seems counterintuitive.

- ⚜ By doing so, you can decrease sales and marketing costs and dramatically improve profitability.

- ⚜ You will also find that instead of feeling out of sync, you'll wake up excited about what you're doing and whom you're working with.

Testing Before Implementing

Robert Sutton

Professor of Management Science and Engineering,
Stanford University

THIS LESSON, ABOUT the employee
courtesy craze at 7-Eleven, is part of what
is a theme throughout my career, which is
the notion that if you have just a little bit of
evidence, you might make better decisions
when you run an organization, rather than
having no evidence at all and just acting on

raw enthusiasm. I think enthusiasm's great, but it's amazing how firms will sometimes move forward on beliefs and won't even test their ideas.

This little story goes back to when I was a new assistant professor and one of my best friends had gotten a job at the 7-Eleven corporation. The parent corporation is The Southland Corporation, and they operate all over the world the little convenience stores that you walk into. This was during what they called the "In Search of Excellence" craze, when just about every manager was obsessed with [Thomas] Peters's and [Robert] Waterman's book.

One of the ideas was that you were supposed to be "close to the customers." In concert with this, the CEO and the primary shareholder in the firm walk into a 7-Eleven and get rude treatment. [The CEO had] read *In Search of Excellence*, and he went back to corporate headquarters and started ranting about the fact that he'd received this rude treatment and that it was driving people out.

Testing Before Implementing

The Southland Corporation, without really testing anything, starts going just insane about trying to improve the quality of courtesies in stores. It was very specific. There were four behaviors: greet, eye contact, smile, and say, "Thank you." There was a little box [on the forms at store registers] for rudeness, but they actually didn't measure much of that because there wasn't much rudeness. They put all these financial incentives and programs in place to get clerks to do those four behaviors, and they put the four behaviors on every 7-Eleven cash register. To show you how dramatic it was, some of the incentives for what I believe are called regional managers— or people to whom many 7-Eleven stores reported—had 30 to 40 percent of their compensation for the year linked to their courtesy scores.

Then they had a contest, which was my favorite part, called the "Thanks a Million" contest, where the owners or managers of 7-Eleven stores who received perfect courtesy [scores] would enter a regional contest, and there'd be a drawing, and then another drawing. In the end they had a drawing in Texas, and they had Monty Hall from the show *Let's Make a Deal*. They drew the name of a woman who ran a store in Plano, Texas, out of the hat: she won a million dollars for the quality of the courtesy in her 7-Eleven stores.

While all of this was going on and millions of dollars were being spent on this, there was a question that my buddy Larry Ford, who was then head of corporate research, and some of us who were also doing research were asking: was this really worth the money to 7-Eleven?

We were doing some experiments, and 7-Eleven was collecting some data. It actually turned out, both from the experiments we were doing and also from some other robust data they had collected, that there was no causal link between the quality of service in the 7-Eleven store and how much they sold.

What would happen would be that, first of all, people did not want rude service.

Testing Before Implementing

Probably to anyone's amazement, it turned out that people just wanted to get in and out of a convenience store quickly. That's what they cared about.

The main thing that drove courtesy in the stores was how long the lines were. When the lines were long—so therefore they were making more money—the clerks would get grumpy and the customers would have fewer expectations for having good, versus bad, service. It's like if you go on an airplane ride and there are six flight attendants and twenty-five passengers, you expect the attendants to stop and be nicer to you. When it's completely crowded, you don't expect them to stop and be nice to you. That was the main finding after [7-Eleven spent] all this money.

It's one of those things that made us realize, moving forward to the lesson, that sometimes instead of catching an idea like a religious fever—like the quality movement or, in this case, the courtesy movement—maybe organizations should stop and do two things. One, do a real experiment, actually do a little test to see if it works; and two, do a pilot program if it's not feasible.

— · —

TAKEAWAYS

— · —

- ⚐ It's great to have enthusiasm in an organization, but only if the ideas and beliefs are tested.

- ⚐ When you have evidence for the strategy you're undertaking, you make better decisions and avoid wasting money on things that don't matter.

- ⚐ Organizations should always test their ideas with real experiments or pilot programs.

Profiting from Evidence-Based Management

Jeffrey Pfeffer

Thomas D. Dee II Professor of Organizational Behavior, Graduate School of Business, Stanford University

MANY ORGANIZATIONS IN today's world make policies and decisions without any concern for the evidence that has been accumulated. It's just astounding to me, and that's why Bob [Robert Sutton] and I wrote this book *Hard Facts, Dangerous Half-Truths,*

Making Strategy Work

and Total Nonsense and are trying to start an evidence-based management movement.

I can give you lots of examples. One example is sitting at a compensation committee meeting of a board of directors and listening to this guy talk about how we needed to basically do the same thing that he had done at his previous company, even though the company that we were talking about had a different product market strategy, was selling different kinds of software to a different customer base, and was a different size. Everything was different, but we're going to take the past into the future.

Another example would be, again, in the area of compensation. People believe in the efficacy of individual incentives. On compensation committees, people will so often say, "We have to have individual pay for performance. We have to have stock options awarded on an individual basis, based upon differences in people's ability to perform." But when you ask them, "Is there any systematic evidence that stock options enhance organizational performance or that individual pay for performance works?" the answer is always, "We know it does."

This kind of emphasis on belief, rather than evidence, gets organizations—and, for that matter, individuals—into trouble all the time. The way to implement evidence-based management is to recognize that, first of all, this is a way of thinking. It's not just a set of techniques. One of the aspects of the way of thinking is to be committed to making decisions based upon the facts.

DaVita, a large kidney dialysis company in the United States, is so committed to fact-based decision making that they send each of their facility administrators a report that shows a bunch of things—costs, treatment outcomes, use of supplies, labor hours, and a bunch of other things. But on that report, if there's an important dimension that would help the facility administrators run the centers better and their information system does not currently produce that information, they put the chart up there anyway, with the words "Not Available." They do that because, in the words of their chief operating officer, Joe Mello, "If we continually tell people that there's an important measure that isn't available, after a while, they figure out how to get it." That really demonstrates a commitment to trying to make decisions, to the extent possible, based upon the facts.

A second thing you ought to obviously do is not pay so much attention to your own personal experience. We have a colleague, Andy Hargadon, who teaches at UC Davis, who says sometimes, "Twenty years of experience is not twenty years of experience. It's one year of experience repeated twenty times." I think people oftentimes infer too much from their own experience, just as doctors sometimes infer too much from their own clinical experience. Therefore, it is incumbent upon managers, just as it is now incumbent upon physicians, to understand what the literature says, to understand what the research says about some practice that they're trying to implement, and not just rely on their own particular kind of judgments and insights.

The implication of this for managers is really two things. First, evidence ought to trump ideology. Second, you really do need to be committed to facts and fact-based decision making. As Gary Loveman, the chief executive officer of Harrah's Entertainment, said, "There are three ways to get fired at Harrah's: sexual harassment, theft, or doing something without running an experiment."

I think companies really need to look at their organizations as unfinished prototypes, and to do what Yahoo! does on its Web site, which is run literally hundreds of experiments a day to see what works and what doesn't. That strikes me as something that is really very essential to implement evidence-based management.

———————◆———————

TAKEAWAYS

———————◆———————

- ⮝ Many organizations make policies and decisions without regard to evidence and instead develop their strategies around untested beliefs, a practice that leads to trouble.

⊨ To implement evidence-based management, companies must be committed to making decisions based upon facts, and employees must stop relying on their own judgments and insights.

⊨ Companies should instead view their organizations as unfinished prototypes and conduct experiments to see what works and what doesn't.

Aligning Strategy Across Multiple Business Units

Stuart Grief

*Vice President of Strategy and Business Development,
Textron*

WORKING STRATEGY AS an enterprise
that has multiple business units is a pretty
tricky thing, because we're always trying
to strike a balance between autonomy of
the business units. At the end of the day,
they're the ones that are closer to their

customers and know best what they ought to be doing, versus maintaining consistency across the businesses.

[Here are] a couple of examples. I've worked with financial services in my consulting days. In a financial services company, where the products on the surface might seem similar, they can run into the trap of one size fits all and having more of a peanut-butter approach to measuring and strategizing within those companies.

In one experience I was working with a company that focused on lending, and they expanded into insurance, as an insurance brokerage firm. They were trying to measure themselves in insurance brokerage by using the same metrics that they used for loans and trying to figure out how to measure charge-offs in an insurance business. Clearly, it just didn't make sense. That's an obvious example of where trying to force a consistent approach doesn't make sense.

At the same time, however, we are looking for some consistency, some balance across the businesses, because, at the center, we are ultimately doing resource allocation between the businesses.

What we've tried to do at Textron, across our businesses, is focus on a small number of high-level lenses that we look through. One, in particular, relates to value creation. That's something that is a universal lens that you can look through at any business and use as a basis for allocating resources from capital to time across the businesses in the portfolio. That's one element where we strive for alignment.

Another place where we strive for alignment is simply on facts that we use within the businesses. For example, about three years ago, I was reviewing strategies with a couple of our businesses. One of our businesses was making the assumption that for the next three years steel prices would continue to rise, while another business unit was making the exact opposite assumption: that over the next three years steel prices would fall. For both businesses it was an important cost component, and, clearly, one of them had to be wrong. Even if both were

wrong or both were right, at least we would
be consistent in our views and could at least
understand the impact of being wrong.

One of the things that I've found very
helpful for us to do at the center of the
company is to at least provide a common set
of planning assumptions that the businesses
ought to be using. What's likely to be happening with overall economic activity in the
countries that we operate in? What's likely
to happen with commodity prices? What's
likely to happen with respect to geopoliti-
cal risk in the various countries where we
operate?

I think that that's a valuable thing for the
center of any company to do for its businesses. Get that off the table so that, A,
the assumptions are consistent and, B, the
business units get more time to focus on
what it is that they do best, which is focusing
on their customers and their products.

A final key learning I would offer in
terms of ensuring alignment is doing all we
can to keep strategy and finance aligned.
My experience is that when the finance

organization and strategy organization aren't working closely together, the likelihood of getting a strategy implemented diminishes dramatically.

As an example, I can reflect on a very specific meeting with one of our business units where a great idea was put forth. By all accounts, it was really a terrific strategy to pursue. There were investment implications, but those had not been brought forth. In any event, finance was not deeply involved in that dialogue. Although the strategy was approved, just by the dialogue and by show of hands, at the end of the day when a formal request for capital was put forth, the finance organization simply didn't recognize it. Therefore, a lot of back pressure was put on this particular business. Things slowed down, and ultimately things changed pretty dramatically.

What we have today is a much more integrated process, where strategy and finance work very closely together. As part of our strategy dialogue process, the finance organization is very deeply involved. They see, in the course of the strategy dialogue, what the likely investment requirements are going to be.

I'd say there are three takeaways from me in trying to achieve alignment across multiple business units. The first is not trying to assert too many metrics that are common across the businesses, because even in businesses that appear similar on the surface, there are typically some pretty fundamental differences.

I think a second takeaway is to help the businesses by providing them some of the key external planning assumptions. It frees up their time, number one. And then, number two, it just keeps businesses from making plans based on differing assumptions that could be pretty wildly different.

The final key takeaway from me on alignment is ensuring that the finance organization and strategy organization are working closely together to keep potential roadblocks downstream with funding from blocking implementation of a particular strategy.

TAKEAWAYS

- ☖ Implementing strategy across a business with multiple and varied business units is tricky but attainable.

- ☖ To align business units with strategy, companies must consider value creation when allocating resources and must base decisions on facts.

- ☖ Further, organizations must integrate the strategy and business functions to prevent funding roadblocks after strategy decisions are made.

Matching People to Strategy

Domenico De Sole

Former President and CEO, Gucci Group

THERE SHOULD BE a strong match in any company that wants to be successful between the human resources that are needed to achieve a certain goal and the strategy.

I'll give you an example. I felt very strongly back in 1993 that to resurrect the company we needed to take more of a "fashion" course to make sure that the

Making Strategy Work

consumers understood what we were trying to do with Gucci—rejuvenating it, making it more exciting and repositioning the brand.

I took a calculated risk, but I had a sense, with Tom Ford and some of the other people, that we had really strong fashion designers. In deciding the strategy to follow, it was obviously very much in my mind that we had the right firepower to make the strategy work.

I think that Tom is a genius; he's brilliant, and we're very close friends who've worked together for a long time. The reality is that the real power is the brand. Obviously, having a strong person who drives the brand inspires the brand. Tom has been fantastic, but I still believe that at the end of the day, the key thing is the underlying brand and the strength of the name recognition of the brand.

Every time we acquire a new brand we always try to find out, "What is the strategy we want to pursue?" Once we've decided the strategy, it becomes very important to pursue the appropriate people, to say,

Matching People to Strategy

"Who do we need?" Obviously we want to be like the Dallas Cowboys in the 1980s; you want to hire the superstars, that is true, but by the same token you have to make sure that the superstars fit within the strategy of the brand.

I'll give you an example. We have a brand called Bottega Veneta that has now started performing extremely well. We made a very clear decision at the beginning with Tom Ford that we wanted to give Bottega Veneta a position as a more classic company: beautifully crafted and a more classic product. With that in mind, we selected a gentleman named Tomas Maier, who's a former creative director of Hermès.

So he had a great understanding of the tradition of the brand and, most importantly, the kind of taste and ability that were consistent with what we wanted to do with it. I think the reason this brand has been doing so well in the last couple of years is because it was a perfect match between the strategy that we put in place and the people driving the strategy.

TAKEAWAYS

⛨ For any company to be successful, a strong match must exist between the strategy and the human resources needed to achieve the goal.

⛨ The real power is in the brand, and it's critical to have a strong person to drive and inspire the brand.

⛨ Once a strategy is in place, organizations must put in place "superstars" who fit within the brand strategy.

Satisfying Your Customers

Sir John Egan

Former Chief Executive, BAA

I'VE ALWAYS THOUGHT that the fundamental purpose behind a business is to make profits by satisfying customers. If you explain to your workforce what you're trying to do, I think that's a wonderful starting point.

When I went to Jaguar, it was in a very powerless state; it was losing 30 percent of net sales, and you really have to try hard to lose that much money. I was trying to get something that would bring the whole company together. I explained that the whole purpose was to create cars of such quality that the customers would be happy and satisfied with them. Everybody in the company knew the processes we had in place to ask our customers whether they were happy or not with the car's performance and quality.

We put in place an absolutely indisputable measure of quality. Then we implemented processes to improve the quality. Once we'd done that and made it easy to make the cars, because the quality was good, productivity almost automatically followed behind.

I went to BAA after running Jaguar, and I was quite clear that satisfying customers was an absolutely core thing to do. While you're learning a new business, you wonder which of your tricks from the past you should carry with you. Satisfying customers was clearly one that was core to my philosophy.

Satisfying Your Customers

I started a process of a customer satisfaction index, where we were constantly talking to passengers about every process they went through, to see what they were and weren't happy with. This then informed the management about what they were doing well and badly.

The strategies of how to run the company came out of this kind of information. Interestingly, one of the things that we were doing worst of all was shopping. People saw the airport as a rip-off; every summer, newspaper reporters went to our airports and bought things very expensively. The "rip-offs" at the airport made huge headlines. It was the worst and least satisfactory of the things that we did.

We put together a retailing program to satisfy the customer, which turned out to be immensely profitable. You're probably now familiar with all the shopping malls that you see not only at BAA airports, but at airports all over the world. It all started from satisfying the customer.

Making Strategy Work

I think a simple view of what you're trying to do in your business—to make profit by satisfying customers—is a message that can be understood by your workforce; they can join in helping you to run the company. They know precisely what you're trying to do. Then your staff can help you in that fundamental mission. They understand what they're doing, and they understand why they're there. Once you get the quality right, you can then start to tackle productivity and improve that as well.

TAKEAWAYS

- ⚔ A central purpose of business is to create profits through customer satisfaction.

- ⚔ To satisfy customers, companies must develop an indisputable measure of quality that is then backed by processes to improve quality.

- ✄ Let customer feedback inform and drive your management. Then share feedback with your workers so that they can join you and execute your strategy.

Stick to Business Principles

John Whybrow

Chairman, Wolseley

I WAS ASKED, as a young manager, to take the responsibility to find a solution to a local problem. It was difficult for the people involved—unions, managers, and workers—and in that circumstance I found that everybody gave me advice. So here was I, a young manager, not quite sure what to do but knowing I had to find a solution.

I talked to various people: my boss, my boss's boss, my peer group, the guys running the shop floor, and several unions. Every time I talked to somebody, there was a barrier. I found myself in the middle with no room to move.

I thought, "What the hell do I do now?" Everybody gave me different advice and views, which conflicted with other views. There was no solution if I tried to please people. Then at three o'clock in the morning, I suddenly realized what to do: you just ignore the advice and decide to use business principles.

I took their view into account, but I didn't let it stop me from making a decision, and we solved the problem. It was solved with everybody having some feeling that they'd been listened to, but equally they knew that their view would not be the prevailing view at the end of the day.

Stick to Business Principles

There's no truism; there's no perfect solution. You have to, therefore, apply your view of those business principles. I think that is defined by your own morality, integrity, objectivity—grand words, but you have to have these things. You apply your own level and view of the world to those business principles. Applying those philosophical values—plus the point that we are here to find a business solution without favor, without politics, and to take those things out—is the fundamental issue.

Stick to business principles. Decide what's right from a business point of view. That way, you find solutions that are respected. You can't please everybody—you never can. I think that's a lesson I learned and subsequently applied myself. As we've gone through time, I have given that advice to some of my guys. If it gets too complicated, stick to business principles and find the business solution. You'll get respect and results.

TAKEAWAYS

◄ To solve a problem, it's natural to seek advice, but too much advice can stifle your ability to find a solution.

◄ When you're inundated with conflicting advice, ignore the advice and instead stick to business principles.

◄ Finding solutions that are right for the business but that reflect your own integrity and objectivity earns you respect and delivers results.

ABOUT THE CONTRIBUTORS

Sanjiv Ahuja is the Chairman of Orange UK, one of the world's leading communications companies. He is also Chairman and CEO of Augere, a new venture aiming to provide broadband access for all.

Mr. Ahuja earned his degree in electrical engineering from Delhi University, India, and his master's in computer science from Columbia University, New York.

He started his career in 1979 as a software engineer at IBM, where he stayed for fifteen years, fulfilling various executive roles, the most senior of which included the responsibility of leading IBM's entry into the telecommunications software industry.

Mr. Ahuja moved on to become President of Telcordia Technologies, Inc. (formerly Bellcore), the world's largest provider of operations support systems, network software, and consulting and engineering services to the telecommunications industry. He then became CEO of Comstellar Technologies, Inc., a California-based technology company.

In April 2003 Mr. Ahuja joined Orange as Chief Operating Officer, moving up to CEO of the Group in March 2004. He stepped down as CEO in April 2007 to pursue other ventures. He continues with the Group as Chairman of Orange UK.

About the Contributors

He is a former member of France Telecom's Group Management Committee. Mr. Ahuja became Director of Cadbury Schweppes, Plc., in May 2006.

David Brandon is the Chairman and CEO of Domino's Pizza PMC, Inc., a world leader in pizza delivery that operates in the United States and in international markets.

Mr. Brandon started his career at Procter & Gamble, where he worked in sales management.

In 1979, following his tenure at Procter & Gamble, Mr. Brandon moved to Valassis, Inc., a company in the sales promotion and coupon industries. He became President and CEO in 1989, a position he held until 1998, while additionally taking on the role of Chairman in the last two years.

Mr. Brandon subsequently moved to Domino's Pizza, where he has been the company's Chairman and CEO since March 1999. In addition to this leadership role, Mr. Brandon has been a Director of Burger King Corporation since 2003, The TJX Companies, Inc., since 2001, and Kaydon Corp. since 2004.

A former University of Michigan football player, Mr. Brandon is also on the university's Board of Regents.

Mary Cantando is the Founder of WomanBusinessOwner.com, a national advisory firm that focuses on helping women-owned businesses expand.

About the Contributors

Ms. Cantando has more than twelve years of experience as an entrepreneurial executive, and she has spent several years researching women business owners. She is a nationally recognized expert on growing women-owned businesses.

Ms. Cantando serves on the National Board of the Women Presidents' Organization and the National Women's Forum of the Women's Business Enterprise National Council, and she is certified by the Women's Business Enterprise National Council. She also serves as the Business Growth Expert for Women Entrepreneurs, Inc.

Ms. Cantando is the author of *The Woman's Advantage: 20 Women Entrepreneurs Show You What It Takes to Grow Your Business* and *Nine Lives: Stories of Women Business Owners Landing on Their Feet*.

Clayton Christensen is the Robert and Jane Cizik Professor of Business Administration at the Harvard Business School, with a joint appointment in the Technology & Operations Management and General Management faculty groups. His research and teaching interests center on managing innovation and creating new growth markets. He has been a faculty member since 1992.

A seasoned entrepreneur, Professor Christensen has founded three successful companies. The first, CPS Corporation, is an advanced materials manufacturing company that he founded in 1984 with several MIT professors. The second, Innosight, is a consulting and training company focused on problems of strategy, innovation, and growth that

About the Contributors

Christensen founded with several of his former students in 2000. Innosight Capital, the third firm, was launched in 2005. From 1979 to 1984, Professor Christensen worked with The Boston Consulting Group, Inc. (BCG). In 1982 he was named a White House Fellow and served as assistant to U.S. Transportation Secretaries Drew Lewis and Elizabeth Dole.

Professor Christensen holds a BA with highest honors in economics from Brigham Young University (1975), and an MPhil in applied econometrics and the economics of less-developed countries from Oxford University (1977), where he studied as a Rhodes Scholar. He received an MBA with High Distinction from the Harvard Business School in 1979, graduating as a George F. Baker Scholar. He was awarded his DBA from the Harvard Business School in 1992.

Professor Christensen is the author or coauthor of five books, and his writings have won a number of awards.

Jay Conger is the Henry Kravis Research Chair Professor, Kravis Leadership Institute at Claremont McKenna College.

Professor Conger is widely acknowledged as one of the world's experts on leadership. He has done extensive research into leadership, boards of directors, organizational change, and the training and development of leaders and managers.

Prior to his academic career Professor Conger worked in government and as an international marketing manager for a high-technology company.

After moving into academia Professor Conger became a research scientist at the Center for Effective Organizations at the University of Southern California. He then became the Executive Director of its Leadership Institute.

Professor Conger was subsequently invited to join London Business School in 1999 in the role of Professor of Organizational Behavior. He remained there until he took his current position at Claremont McKenna College in 2005. Harvard Business School has also asked him to help redesign its organizational behavior course around leadership issues.

Additionally, Professor Conger has been involved in executive education at INSEAD, one of the world's leading and largest graduate business schools.

An accomplished writer, he has written or cowritten more than ten books and one hundred scholarly articles. His titles include *Shared Leadership: Reframing the How's and Why's of Leading Others* and *Winning 'Em Over: A New Model for Managing in the Age of Persuasion*. His latest book, *The Practice of Leadership: Developing the Next Generation of Leaders*, examines what top scholars consider the best practices of leadership in numerous sectors.

In addition to his academic work, Professor Conger consults for a number of private corporations and nonprofit organizations worldwide.

About the Contributors

Domenico De Sole is the former President and CEO of Gucci Group NV, a leading multibrand luxury goods company.

Mr. De Sole moved from Italy to the United States in 1970, where he earned a master's degree from Harvard University and became a partner in the Washington law firm of Patton, Boggs & Blow. He joined Gucci in 1984 as CEO of Gucci America. He remained in New York until 1994, when he moved to Italy as Gucci Group's Chief Operating Officer.

He was appointed CEO, and at the end of 1995 led Gucci Group's listing on the New York and Amsterdam stock exchanges. In 1999 he successfully fought a hostile takeover bid, securing Gucci's independence as a basis for continued expansion, which has included the acquisition of Yves Saint Laurent, Alexander McQueen, and Stella McCartney.

Mr. De Sole left Gucci in 2004. The same year he joined the board of Gap Inc. He is also Director of Bausch & Lomb, Inc.; Telecom Italia, S.p.A; and Delta Air Lines.

Sir John Egan is the former Chief Executive of BAA, the world's leading airport company, in charge of day-to-day security, retail, strategy, investment, and more. Currently, he serves as Chancellor of Coventry University, a position to which he was appointed in March 2007.

From 1968 to 1990, Sir John developed a successful career in the automotive industry, working for General Motors Corporation and British Leyland and rising to become Chairman and Chief Executive of Jaguar in May 1980.

Sir John joined British Leyland as Chairman of Jaguar Cars, Ltd. When Jaguar was privatized in August 1984 he remained as Chairman and Chief Executive. After the takeover by Ford Motor Company, Sir John retired from Jaguar and was appointed to the Board of Directors of BAA in June 1990, taking up the position of Chief Executive in September 1990, a position he held until October 1999.

Sir John was also Chairman of the Construction Task Force. Its report "Rethinking Construction" was commissioned by the Deputy Prime Minister, John Prescott, and was published in July 1998.

Sir John is a former Chairman of Inchcape Shipping Services, a marine services provider; Harrison Lovegrove & Co., an oil and gas corporate finance advisory firm; and Asite Solutions, Ltd., whose product portfolio includes tools for collaboration, trading, and sourcing. He joined the board of the environmental services group Severn Trent, Plc., in October 2004 and became Chairman in January 2005.

Lynda Gratton is the Professor of Management Practice at the London Business School. In this role she directs the school's executive program Human Resource Strategy in Transforming Organizations.

A trained psychologist, Ms. Gratton worked for the global airline British Airways for several years as

About the Contributors

an occupational psychologist, and then became Director of HR Strategy at PA Consulting Group.

She is a prolific author and from 1992 to 2002 she led the Leading Edge Research Consortium.

Ms. Gratton serves on the Board of the Concours Group and on the Editorial Review Board of *People & Strategy*, the journal of the Human Resource Planning Society. She conducts CEO, CIO, and HR Director workshops in the United Kingdom and the United States. She also consults with multinationals, including Shell, Unilever, Royal Bank of Scotland, and Hewlett-Packard Development Company, Ltd.

In 2007 Ms. Gratton was included in the *Times*'s list of the top fifty business thinkers in the world.

Stuart Grief is the Vice President of Strategy and Business Development at Textron, Inc., one of the world's largest and most successful multi-industry companies.

Prior to joining Textron, Mr. Grief served as Vice President and Director at The Boston Consulting Group, Inc. (BCG). During his fourteen-year tenure, he was a senior member of the U.S. Industrial Goods and Automotive practices and a leader of the Corporate Finance and Strategy practice. His expertise in the areas of business development, market and portfolio strategy, and operations includes client work in market segmentation, growth strategies, and restructuring and business

integration. He also led BCG's recruiting activities
in Boston for five years.

In July 2004, Mr. Grief joined Textron. As
Vice President of Strategy and Business Development, he works closely with senior leadership across
the enterprise to create and implement business
unit and corporate strategies that drive growth,
profitability, and shareholder value creation. In
addition, Mr. Grief is a corporate officer and a
member of the Transformation Leadership Team.

Philip Kotler is the S.C. Johnson & Son Professor
of International Marketing at the Kellogg School of
Management, Northwestern University.

Professor Kotler is the author of several books,
including *Marketing Management: Analysis, Planning, Implementation and Control*, the most widely used marketing
book in graduate business schools worldwide. He
has published more than one hundred articles in
leading journals, several of which have received
best-article awards.

Professor Kotler has consulted for such companies as IBM Corporation; General Electric Company; AT&T Corporation; Honeywell
International, Inc.; Bank of America Corporation;
Merck & Co., Inc.; and others in the areas of
marketing strategy and planning, marketing organization, and international marketing.

He has been Chairman of the College of Marketing of the Institute of Management Sciences, a

About the Contributors

Director of the American Marketing Association, a Trustee of the Marketing Science Institute, Director of the MAC Group, a former member of the Yankelovich Advisory Board, and a member of the Copernicus Advisory Board. He is a member of the Board of Governors of the School of the Art Institute of Chicago and a member of the Advisory Board of the Drucker Foundation.

Roger Parry is the former Chairman and CEO of Clear Channel International, the world's leading out-of-home media company operating across radio, outdoor advertising, and live entertainment.

Mr. Parry spent the first seven years of his career as a reporter and producer, working for the BBC and commercial television and radio. He then became a consultant with McKinsey & Company, where he had a range of clients across marketing strategy and post-merger integration.

He moved on to become Development Director of Aegis Group, Plc., a marketing communications company. In this role he was part of the team that managed the successful restructuring and refinancing of Aegis in 1992.

He was CEO of More Group, Inc., from 1995 to 1998, when it was acquired by Clear Channel. Parry was CEO of Clear Channel International for six years. He became Chairman in 2004 and left in 2005.

In July 2007, Mr. Parry became Executive Chairman of the marketing communications group

About the Contributors

Media Square, Plc. He is currently Chairman of newspaper publisher Johnston Press, Plc., and Mobile Streams, Plc. He is former Chairman of the magazine group Future, Plc.

Jeffrey Pfeffer is the Thomas D. Dee II Professor of Organizational Behavior at the Graduate School of Business, Stanford University.

Professor Pfeffer has taught at Stanford University since 1979. He is the author or coauthor of eleven books, including *The Human Equation: Building Profits by Putting People First*; *Managing with Power: Politics and Influence in Organizations*; *The Knowing–Doing Gap: How Smart Companies Turn Knowledge into Action*; and *Hidden Value: How Great Companies Achieve Extraordinary Results with Ordinary People*. His most recent book, *Hard Facts, Dangerous Half-Truths, and Total Nonsense: Profiting from Evidence–Based Management*, is coauthored with Robert Sutton.

Professor Pfeffer began his career at the Business School at the University of Illinois and then taught at the University of California, Berkeley. He has also been a visiting professor at the Harvard Business School.

He served on the board of Unicru, Inc. (acquired by Kronos, Inc., in August 2006). Currently serving on the board of directors of Audible Magic and SonoSite, Inc. (SONO), Professor Pfeffer consults to, and provides executive education for, numerous companies, associations, and universities in the United States. He also writes a monthly column on management issues titled

About the Contributors

"The Human Factor" for the business magazine *Business 2.0*.

Robert Sutton is the Professor of Management Science and Engineering at Stanford University. At Stanford he co-leads the Center for Work, Technology and Organization and is a faculty member in the Stanford Technology Ventures Program.

A former Professor of Haas Business School, he has been at Stanford since joining in 1983 after completing his PhD at the University of Michigan. During the past twenty years, he has been developing the simple core message that long-term performance is dependent on having a number of good ideas that are subsequently implemented.

A prolific writer, Professor Sutton has authored *The Knowing-Doing Gap*; *Weird Ideas that Work*; and *Hard Facts, Dangerous Half-Truths, and Total Nonsense: Profiting from Evidence-Based Management*, coauthored with Jeffrey Pfeffer.

Professor Sutton teaches in Stanford's professional education program. He also consults with a number of global blue-chip companies, including Ernst & Young Global Ltd.; Gap, Inc.; Hewlett-Packard Development Company, Ltd.; IBM Corporation; McDonald's Corporation; PepsiCo, Inc.; Procter & Gamble; and Xerox Corporation.

He has been a Fellow of the Center for Advanced Study in the Behavioral Sciences in 1986–1987, 1994–1995, and 2002–2003.

About the Contributors

John Whybrow is the Chairman of Wolseley, Plc., a leading distributor of heating and plumbing products and a leading supplier of building materials and services.

Mr. Whybrow's career started at the English Electric Company in 1968. He originally joined Philips in 1970, rising to become Managing Director of the Philips Power Semiconductors and Microwave business in 1987.

In 1993 he was appointed Chairman and Managing Director of Philips Electronics UK. He was then made President and CEO of Philips Lighting Holding in Holland.

From May 1998 until April 2002, he held the post of Executive Vice President of Royal Philips Electronics, where he also took Board responsibility for leading quality and e-business initiatives within the company.

Mr. Whybrow first joined Wolseley as a Director in 1997 and is now its Chairman. He also has been a Director of the consumer electronics retailer Dixons (DSG International, Plc.) since 2003.

⊰ ACKNOWLEDGMENTS ⊱

First and foremost, a heartfelt thanks goes to all of the executives who have candidly shared their hard-earned experience and battle-tested insights for the Lessons Learned series.

Angelia Herrin at Harvard Business School Publishing consistently offered unwavering support, good humor, and counsel from the inception of this ambitious project.

Brian Surette, Hollis Heimbouch, and David Goehring provided invaluable editorial direction, perspective, and encouragement. Much appreciation goes to Jennifer Lynn for her research and diligent attention to detail. Many thanks to the entire HBSP team of designers, copy editors, and marketing professionals who helped bring this series to life.

Finally, thanks to our fellow cofounder James MacKinnon and the entire Fifty

Acknowledgments

Lessons team for the tremendous amount of time, effort, and steadfast support for this project.

—Adam Sodowick
   Andy Hasoon
   Directors and Cofounders
   Fifty Lessons